ALL ABOUT DIVORCE

by Mary Blitzer Field
Illustrated by Alex Forbes
Foreword by Lawrence E. Shapiro, Ph.D.

D1361556

The Center for Applied Psychology
King of Prussia, Pennsylvania

All About Divorce

by Mary Blitzer Field
Illustrated by Alex Forbes
Play-and-Read Series Editor: Hennie M. Shore
Concept by Lawrence E. Shapiro, Ph.D.

Published by:
The Center for Applied Psychology, Inc.
P.O. Box 61587
King of Prussia, PA 19406   USA
Telephone: 215/277-4020

The Center for Applied Psychology, Inc. is the publisher of Childswork/Childsplay, a catalog of products for mental health professionals, teachers, and parents who wish to help children with their social and emotional growth. For information or to obtain a catalog call toll-free 1/800/962-1141.

SECOND PRINTING

© Copyright 1992 by The Center for Applied Psychology, Inc.
Printed in the United States of America.

ISBN 1-882732-00-6

TABLE OF CONTENTS

FOREWORD..V

WHEN TO SEEK PROFESSIONAL HELP...................X

ALL ABOUT THIS BOOK......................................1

WHY DO PARENTS GET DIVORCED......................2

WHAT ABOUT WHEN YOU FEEL SAD?................22

WHAT ABOUT WHEN YOU FEEL AFRAID?..............26

DON'T THEY LOVE ME ANYMORE?......................42

IT'S OK TO FEEL ANGRY....................................48

BEING GOOD WON'T WORK MAGIC....................56

DON T PLAY THE BLAMING GAME......................64

SOME DIVORCE DO'S AND DON'TS......................70

TWENTY VERY IMPORTANT THINGS FOR
KIDS TO REMEMBER..83

DIVORCE WORDS AND WHAT THEY MEAN..............85

ACTIVITIES

WHAT WOULD YOU SAY?..................................89

TELL-A-STORY PAGES......................................101

Family Dolls and Play Scenes are included with this book to facilitate creative play and help children express their feelings about divorce.

Publisher's Note: We regret that due to cost and availability factors, we are limited to including Family Dolls with light skin tone only. We hope that you will substitute other dolls for children of color should the need arise.

FOREWORD

HELPING THE CHILDREN OF DIVORCE

In over a dozen years as a child psychologist, I saw many children whose parents were divorcing. Sometimes the children were very unhappy. Sometimes they acted like they didn't care. Some had an understanding way beyond their years and others were totally overwhelmed. But one thing that they all had in common was that none of them wanted to talk about their parents' divorce.

Unlike adults who seek help, children do not frequently talk about their problems. I can remember many occasions when a parent would say this to his child:

> "Tell Dr. Shapiro how you are feeling."
> Silence.
> *Or,* "Tell Dr. Shapiro what happened yesterday."
> "Nothing much."
> *Or,* "Don't you want Dr. Shapiro to help us sort out our problems?"
> "I don't care."

And that was how far talking got us.

But when given an intermediary device—a book, a puppet, a doll, or a game—children readily talk and listen. These "tools" simultaneously act as a stimulus for children to talk and a buffer which makes them feel safe enough to reveal their inner thoughts and feelings.

Unlike other self-help books on divorce, *All About Divorce* recognizes that learning the facts about the divorcing process is only the first step. Children of divorce must integrate the changes going on in their lives into their sense of self, and this must be done on several levels. *All About Divorce* encourages children to explore their thoughts and feelings on four important developmental levels.

All About Divorce begins with the facts about divorce, told and illustrated simply and sensitively. Even the most well-meaning adults forget how different things are from the viewpoint of a child. We take the simplest and most basic facts for granted, but children often don't have this knowledge or may need it repeated again and again until they comprehend it (see "Twenty Very Important Things for Kids to Remember" on page 84).

Some adults may find the writing or the illustration in this book sad or even depressing. The truth is that divorce is a sad event. We believe that children and adults must face up to the difficult emotions experienced in a divorce in order to proceed to happier times. *All About Divorce* deals with the painful topics rather than skip over them, because the best way to reassure children is with the truth, told in a manner they can comprehend.

Divorce has sometimes been called "a death where nobody dies." Most children will go through a period of "mourning" at some time during the divorce process. Most counselors agree that these feelings are wholly appropriate and should not be denied.

All About Divorce includes a play family and backdrop scenes that can be assembled for children to play out their inner concerns. Doll play allows for the broad expression of feelings so necessary to a child's sense of control over his or her world.

The next set of activities allows the children to give words to their feelings. The book provides ten pictures with "speech balloons" where children must express how different people are feeling.

Finally, the child (or the adult) can write stories related to the divorcing process. You will find six "story starters" and pages on which the child can write or dictate a story. Young children may not be able to tell a very detailed story and may wish to draw instead. Adults may also wish to take this opportunity to make up a story themselves. Children love to have stories written especially for them.

You will notice that each of the "story starters" are positive. While there must be a place and time for children to explore and communicate the negative feelings that accompany divorce, we believe that ultimately these changes in the family can be resolved and accepted. Developing a positive attitude toward oneself and one's family will go a long way toward moving on to the next phase of life.

The following are some suggestions about using the different parts of this book to best help children who are experiencing a divorce.

READING ALL ABOUT DIVORCE

We recommend reading this book with your child, even if the child can read by himself. Some children will want to read the book straight through and others will want to only read a little at a time. Some children will want to skip to the activity parts of the book before they are finished reading and others may not want to do the activities at all.

Above all, take your time. Children need time to learn about divorce and absorb the vast changes in their lives. This book can serve as a reference point for children as they adjust to the new realities of their lives. It provides important facts and information about the divorcing process, and it is our hope that the book will go a long way toward dispelling the common misperceptions of children that can lead them into guilt and self-blame. It can also help to orient adults to the ways that children think and learn about divorce.

Remember that learning about divorce is like learning about anything else it—takes time to absorb the facts. Accepting divorce takes time, too, but patience and an attitude of forgiveness of yourself and others will help.

USING THE FAMILY DOLLS AND PLAY SCENES

We have provided eight backdrops and a play family for children to use to act out family scenes. Adults observing or playing with children should remember that there is no right or wrong way to play. If you observed a classroom of children playing with small dolls or action figures, you would see the entire range of childhood play. Some children say very little. Their dolls move in silence as they enact a pantomime of actions with meaning only to the child. Other children talk constantly. Their dolls chatter back and forth, mimicking real-life conversations or bringing forth a wellspring of ideas and feelings which may surprise the casual observer.

For the most part, children are protective about their magical language of play. They rarely reveal, even though play, that which they do not want to be known. We recommend that you follow the child's lead in participating or observing his doll play just as if you might is you came upon him acting out a scene with dolls on the kitchen table.

If a child seems uncomfortable with your presence during his play, then you should leave him to play by himself. Children need the opportunity to express themselves freely.

If a child is uncomfortable letting you observe him play, then do so quietly and non-judgementally. You can learn a great deal about children by watching them play, but you must remember to respect the boundaries of their inner world. Play is meant to express feelings, and sometimes children will express feelings that make us uncomfortable.

It is important to remember that children in a family that is going through a divorce will have a variety of feelings, even about the people whom they love most. Anger is normal. Sadness is normal. Confusion and contradiction in a child's world is to be expected his play will help him sort things out.

Never take what a child says during play at face value. Remember the story of the mother who repeatedly observed her four-year-old daughter putting a Mommy doll's head in the toilet? The mother watched her daughter doing this over and over again, each time wondering, "Why is my daughter so angry at me? What have I done to deserve being flushed down the toilet?"

Finally, the mother could stand it no longer and asked her child, "Are you angry at Mommy? Why do you keep putting your 'pretend' Mommy in the toilet?" The child answered, "Because I wanted to wash off her make-up and I don't have a 'doll sink.'"

We recommend that you set up the Play Scenes before you begin reading the book with the child. Have the family dolls nearby so that the child may switch to playing if he or she so desires.

Some children want adults to participate in their play; to take the role of one or more dolls. Remember again to follow the child's lead. Play therapists typically use doll play to reflect or mirror what is on a child's mind. If a child's play is casual, then make your play casual. If a child begins expressing feelings or concerns through his or her dolls, then it is wise to simply parrot those concerns.

For example:

> Boy (holding the daddy doll): "I'm leaving now and I don't know when I'll be back."
> Mother (holding the mommy doll): "You don't know if you are coming back?"
> Boy: "That's right. I may be back tonight, though."
> Mother: "You may be back tonight?"
> Boy: "That's right. Maybe."

What is important about this dialogue is *what was not said* by the mother. The boy's mother did not take the opportunity to get in her own "two cents worth" about the real facts or even express her point of view (the father in this family had left in anger one night and was not seen again for nearly a month). She simply restated what her son was saying, giving him the opportunity to express his desire that maybe his father would return.

Children need to work through their reality at their own pace. Adults do confusing things and children need time to understand them. Never make this more difficult for a child by using play to state your own case. It may have been tempting for the mother in the above illustration to express her anger at her husband's leaving or her interpretation of what her child should be feeling. But she wisely kept her feelings to herself.

In doll play, and in other ways that parents interact with their children about divorce, adults must put aside their need to express their own point of view in favor of helping children sort things out for themselves. To learn more about reflective listening, we highly recommend the book *How to Talk So Children Will Listen and Listen So Children Will Talk* by Adele Farber and Elaine Mazlish (Avon Books, New York, 1980).

WHAT WOULD YOU SAY?

As we have noted, the activities in *All About Divorce* present a progression of ways in which children learn to express their feelings about divorce. Doll play is often unorganized and nonverbal, but children must eventually learn to put words to their feelings in a logical and comprehensible manner.

We have provided ten scenes with speech balloons for children to fill in the dialogue about what they think various people are saying to each other. This type of activity requires children to put themselves in another person's shoes (although we recognize that when children take the role of another person, they are revealing their feelings as well).

Again, we advise adults to consider their comments wisely so that they encourage the child to continue expressing feelings, whatever they may be. For example, if a child fills in a speech balloon to say "I hate you, mother," the adult might comment, "That boy is really angry at his mother" rather than saying something like, "Is that how you feel about me?"

An adult is always on safe ground when he or she is simply reflecting or mirroring what the child has already said. If a child reveals feelings or thoughts which are extremely intense or surprising then a parent or teacher should proceed even more cautiously. When intense feelings are very close to the surface, then professional counseling may be indicated. Please refer to the section, "When To Seek Professional Help" on page xiii.

TELL-A-STORY

Finally, we have given the child six stories to write. We have provided only the beginning of the first sentence to start the story.

If children wish to complete the story, they can either write it in the book or dictate it to you. Younger children may wish to draw a picture or two with the story.

If a child does not want to write a story, then you may wish to write one. Make your story short, simple, and positive. Emphasize some of the important points that we have made in this book, but in your own words. Children love to hear or read stories that have been written "just for them." Writing a positive and personalized story for a child will help him or her more than you can imagine.

Divorce affects nearly half of the children in the U.S. In the first year after the divorce, many of the children of divorce will develop the "normal" symptoms of sadness, anxiety, and anger. But before this year is up, all but ten percent will accept the changes that have occurred in their lives. Of this ten percent, some may have lingering problems for years to come, but research has shown that the ones who are most anxious or regressed generally have been exposed to the least amount of information about divorce or have had little opportunity for open communication.

It is our hope that *All About Divorce* will help you open up a dialogue with the children you are concerned about. Divorce has become a fact of life in our society. By being honest and open to change, we can point the way for children toward self-acceptance and growth.

–Lawrence E. Shapiro, Ph.D.

WHEN TO SEEK PROFESSIONAL HELP

It is our belief that many different people can help children with psychological issues. Parents, teachers, grandparents, neighbors, and friends of the family have always been the primary influences on the emotional development of children, through good times and bad. The significant people in a child's life can enhance his natural helping abilities through self-help books and other parenting tools.

But some children need more. A percentage of children whose parents divorce need professional counseling at some time. This may be because of the particular difficulties in the divorcing process, or it may be due to the makeup of the individual child, or it may be both.

There are many people trained to help children and their families through the divorce process. These include psychologists, psychiatrists, social workers, family therapists, pastoral counselors, school psychologists and others. Some of the most common sources of referrals are pediatricians, school principals and school psychologists.

When choosing someone to help you and your children, make sure that he or she has experience in helping families going through a divorce, and make sure that you are comfortable with her. Sometimes a family in crisis selects a helping professional impulsively in order to get some relief as soon as possible. Although it is often difficult, we strongly recommend that you take time in making your decision and that you interview two or three professionals and choose the one whom you feel is most qualified.

It is normal for children whose parents are divorcing to experience a negative reaction. It is normal for them to sometimes express anger, sadness, and anxiety about the future. But a child or family may need professional help if these feelings are unusually intense, are prolonged in duration, cause physical symptoms, or interfere with the normal day-to-day tasks of childhood.

Place a check by any of the following statements that describes a child about whom you are concerned. IF YOU CHECK EVEN ONE OF THESE STATEMENTS, THEN YOU SHOULD CONSULT A MENTAL HEALTH PROFESSIONAL.

PROBLEM CHECKLIST

___The child shows a pronounced loss of appetite, change of sleeping habits, or other disturbance in his day-to-day routine.

___The child seems angry or depressed all the time.

___The child has new difficulties in school, either socially or academically.

___The child is argumentative or defiant.

___The child wishes to be alone most of the time.

___The child displays constant physical symptoms including, but not limited to: stomach aches, tics, constant tiredness, aches and pains, headaches.

___The child has sudden mood swings.

___The child has a very negative view about everything and often says negative things about himself.

___The child shows an unusual degree of worry and anxiety.

Under normal circumstances, most parents would immediately notice any sudden change in their child's behavior, but divorcing parents can be so overwhelmed in their own right, and so many things change so fast, that even significant changes in a child may be overlooked.

If there is any question that your child may need help, we urge you to consult a professional. He or she or he will be the best person to help you evaluate your situation objectively and judge which problems will diminish with time and which need more attention. A helpful book by Norma Doft, Ph.D. is *When Your Child Needs Help: A Parent's Guide to Therapy for Children* (Harmony Books, New York, 1992).

ALL ABOUT THIS BOOK

Not so long ago, you learned that your mom and dad were going to get a divorce. Maybe at first you couldn't believe it. Maybe you also didn't really understand it.

Then, chances are, you felt really awful. Everything felt different, and scary, too. Like many children, you may have tried to make believe that you didn't feel bad, or you may have tried to hide your feelings.

But when you hide your feelings, you're not helping yourself. If you try to hide from your problems, you can't solve them. They may get even worse, and you may begin to feel worse too.

It's much better to know the truth about the things that are bothering you, even though the truth can hurt or be scary. When you know the truth, you can often do something to help yourself.

And that's what this book is all about. You can trust this book because it will tell you the truth. It won't hide things from you. It will tell you all about divorce, and it will help you with what you might be feeling, even if your feelings make you mad, sad or afraid.

It is our wish that this book will help you to help yourself, and to find help from the grownups you trust the most.

WHY DO PARENTS GET DIVORCED?

When your mom and dad got married, they planned to spend the rest of their lives together. They were so happy just being together that they thought they would feel that way forever.

But after a while, they didn't like each other so much anymore.

Some parents fight without saying a word to each other. Others, like yours, have noisy fights when they don't get along.

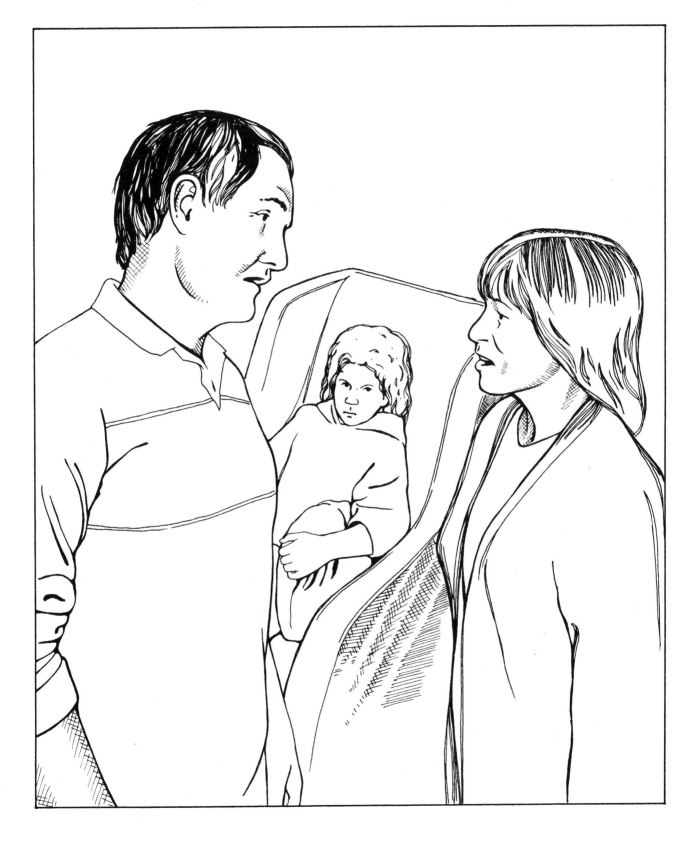

Sometimes parents just can't seem to get along no matter how hard they try, so they decide to live apart from each other. This is called a separation.

During a separation, parents try to figure out what to do about their marriage.

Some parents decide to try to make their marriage work, and they get back together. Others decide that their marriage can't work anymore. They must decide between a bad marriage or no marriage at all.

Kids usually want their parents to stay in a bad marriage rather than have them split up. But parents usually feel that it is best to end a bad marriage. They feel that they would be happier living apart, so they decide to get a divorce.

To make their divorce real and official, parents must ask a judge to write certain things on a paper. The paper says that the mom and dad are no longer married but that they are still the mom and dad of their children.

The paper also has rules about who will take care of the children, and how much time the children will spend with each parent.

Sometimes parents ask lawyers to help them understand the rules or laws about divorce. Parents also ask lawyers to help them if they can't agree with each other. Children can also have their own lawyer.

If you have a lawyer, remember that he or she is on your side, sort of like a friend. If you have to go to court, your lawyer will be there with you. If your lawyer or a judge asks you questions, try to be honest. Your answers will help them to help you.

If your parents have decided to get a divorce, you may hope that they will get back together. You should know that most parents don't. Thinking of ways to bring them back together isn't a great idea, because it hardly ever works. But there are some good ways to help yourself feel better.

For example, don't be afraid to tell your friends that your parents aren't living together anymore. It's really not so strange. Probably lots of your friends have parents who aren't together anymore. And anyway, the main thing kids really care about is whether you're nice and fun to play with.

You may find it easier to tell your friends one by one. This will make your real friends feel good because you trust them with your feelings. And telling your friends will make you feel better too. If you feel angry or sad, tell someone. Don't keep it all inside!

What about someone who teases you? It won't hurt so much if you remember this: Nothing is wrong with you just because your mom and dad are getting divorced.

Maybe your friend is scared that his parents might get a divorce too. Teasing you and trying to make you feel worse might help him feel that divorce is something that can only happen to your family and not his.

You can also help yourself by talking with the grownups you love and trust. You might feel that you want to be alone, but you should let those who love you the most help you. Have you tried talking with your mom or dad?

Many grandparents are good listeners too. So are some are older brothers and sisters. Sometimes neighbors and teachers can be a big help. You can tell your feelings to older people and ask them questions. They usually know the answers that will help you feel better. And it's OK to ask the same questions again and again.

Once in a while, a child may need to talk with a special kind of grownup whose job it is to make people feel better. This grownup is called a counselor (or sometimes a therapist, psychologist, or social worker).

If you visit a counselor, at first you may have a little trouble talking about your feelings with someone you don't know very well. But remember, the counselor needs to know what you're feeling so that he or she can help you.

WHAT ABOUT WHEN YOU FEEL SAD?

Even when children have special grownups to talk to, they usually feel sad after a divorce. Always remember that it's okay to cry! Even older kids and grownups cry sometimes. Crying usually makes you feel better.

For a while, you might think a lot about the parent who is not living with you anymore. If you have thoughts like these, chances are they make you sad. Do you ever have sad feelings that seem to come all of a sudden and knock you over like big waves at the beach? Most people do.

But remember, these thoughts and feelings can help you. If it's your dad who moved out, each time you have a picture of him in your mind, it helps you get used to the fact that he is no longer there. As time goes on, you'll have these thoughts less and less often. You'll always miss your dad, but you'll get used to not having him around as much. This may be hard to believe now, but it will happen. Those sad feelings will grow smaller and smaller, and after a while, they won't be able to knock you down at all.

WHAT ABOUT WHEN YOU FEEL AFRAID?

Besides feeling sad, some children also feel scared. Sometimes when a child learns that his parents are moving apart, he feels like his whole world is falling apart. The ground under his feet may even feel a little shaky.

If you ever feel this way, just remember that your mom is still your mom, and your dad is still your dad, and this will never change. And most important of all is that you are still you, no matter how many changes are going on.

Even when a child remembers these things, she may still worry. She may think, "If my mom left me, then why wouldn't my dad do the same thing?" Or she might think, "Mom didn't want to be around Dad anymore, so she probably doesn't want to be with me anymore either."

But these thoughts just don't make sense. Just because something happened once doesn't mean it will happen again.

Another kind of thinking that doesn't make sense goes like this: "I'm so mad at my mom that I wish she'd get lost for good!" But remember that angry thoughts can't make something happen. So don't be afraid to feel mad!

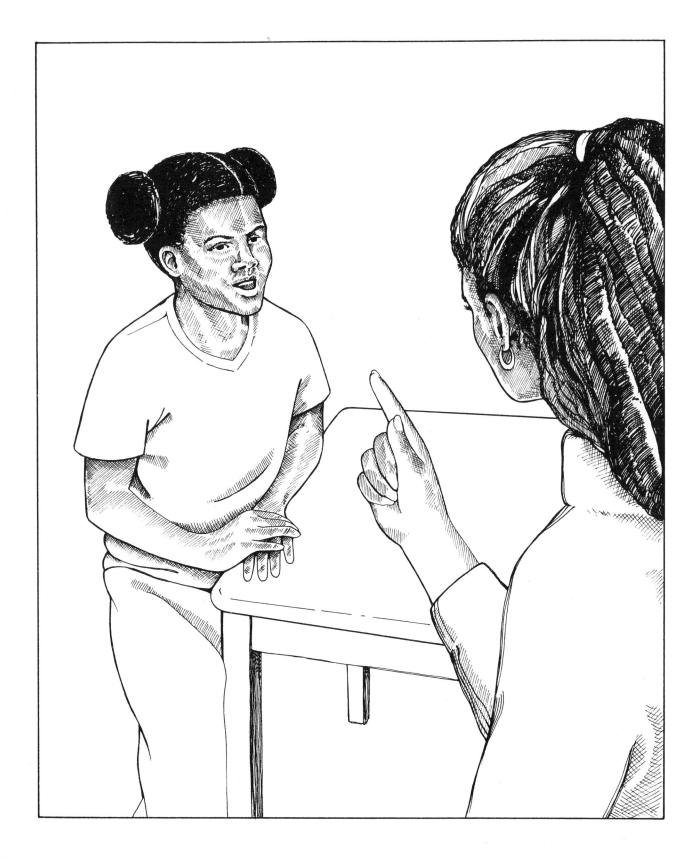

Thinking that the parent you live with might leave may make you worry a lot. Do you ever wonder who will keep you safe, or who will take care of you if you're sick? If you tell your parents or other grownups that you're worried about these kinds of things they'll be able to give you answers that will make you feel better.

Some children worry so much about losing their mom that they always want to be around her. They don't even want to leave her to go to sleep or to school.

You never need to worry about this. You still have two parents, and you always will. If something happened to the parent you live with, your other parent could take care of you. A child can almost always live with one parent or the other.

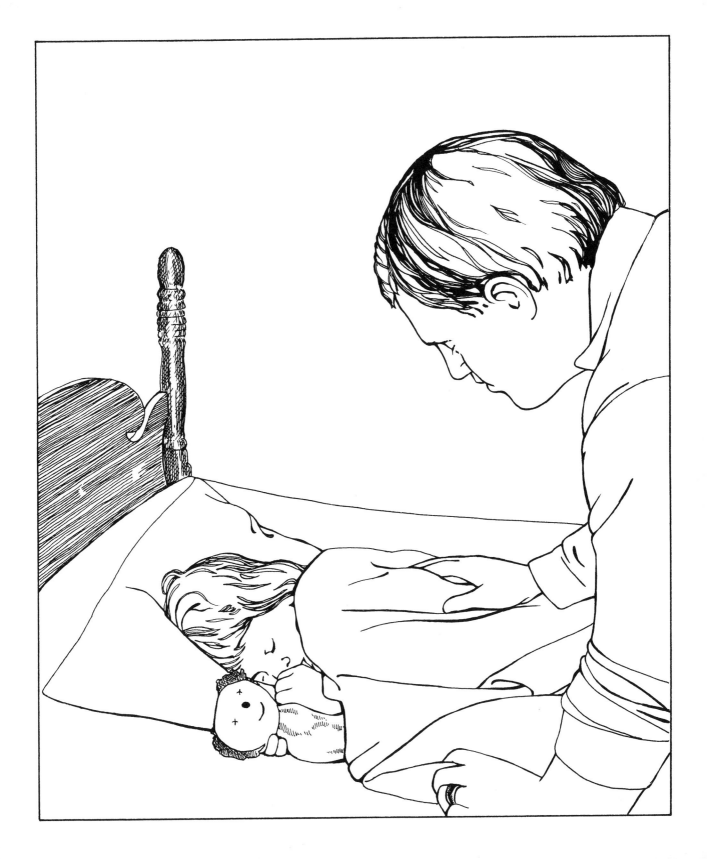

But just suppose you couldn't live with either one of your parents. What would happen then? You could still live with another special grownup who would take care of you, like a grandparent, an aunt, an uncle, a cousin, or even a good friend of your parents.

Ask your parents who would take care of you if neither of them could. It's a good question to ask, you'll feel safer when you know.

Suppose neither parent could take care of you, nor could any other special grownup. Then what? There will always be places where you can go where there are grownups who will take care of you.

For example, you could live at a special kind of school called a boarding school, where you would go to school during the day and sleep at night too. Grownups are at these schools all the time, day and night, and it is their job to take care of the children who live there.

Another place where children can live is in a foster home. Foster parents are regular parents who take care of other children along with their own.

So you can see that, one way or another, there will always be a grownup to take care of you. You will always be safe.

DON'T THEY LOVE ME ANYMORE?

Even if you feel safe, you may still have thoughts that trouble you. Have you ever wondered why your dad left if he still loves you?

Most children who think that the parent who left doesn't love them anymore are wrong. Remember, your dad left because he didn't want to live with your mom anymore. He didn't leave because of you. Chances are, your dad still loves you—a whole lot.

Once in a while it happens that a parent who leaves home doesn't love her children very much, and maybe not at all. How can you tell whether your mom loves you? If she wants to spend time with you, she probably loves you. This doesn't mean that she has to spend all her time or even most of her time with you. Moms and dads have to go to work and take care of the house.

But if a parent almost never makes time to be with you, he may not love you very much. A parent who loves you tries hard to help you if you're sick or in trouble. A parent who loves you will be happy and proud when you learn something new. And he will want to hold and touch you, at least sometimes.

If you think one of your parents doesn't love you, remember that this doesn't mean that other people can't love you. There are lots of things about you to love.

IT'S OK TO FEEL ANGRY

We've already agreed that it's okay to feel angry. People feel mad when they don't get what they want. Most children want their parents to stay together. When parents get divorced, this is almost never what the children want. So they get angry.

But some children are afraid to get angry. They worry that their angry thoughts might hurt the person they're mad at. But just thinking angry thoughts can never hurt another person. And thinking angry thoughts can help you feel better in the long run.

Sometimes letting people know why you're angry can help you. You can use your anger to try to get what you want. Sometimes it will work, and sometimes it won't. For example, telling your dad that you're mad at him for not visiting more often might make him visit more. But it might not.

If getting angry doesn't get you what you want, you should try to think of something else that you want, and then try to get it. Maybe playing with a good friend could make you feel better about not seeing your dad so much. It's usually a waste of time trying to get what you can't have.

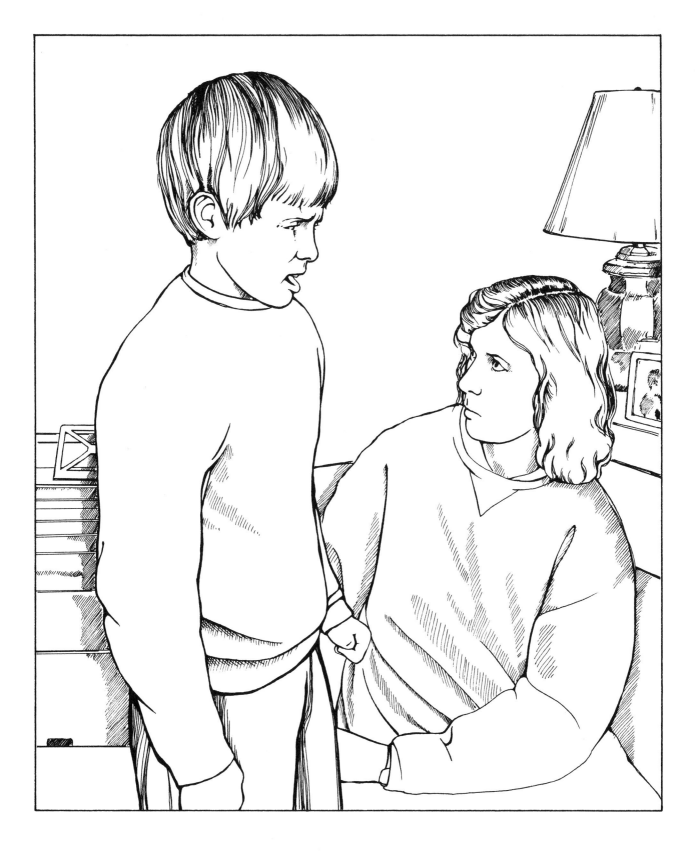

Here's a little story that will help you understand. A dog chased a cat that ran high up into a tree where no on could ever find him—no matter what. Hoping against hope, the dog ran to another tree, thinking the cat might be there.

The dog barked and barked, but there was no sign of the cat. The dog kept hoping and hoping, barking and barking. His barking never made the cat appear. The dog was wasting his time. He was barking up the wrong tree.

Don't you bark up the wrong tree! If you use your anger to try to get what you want, but it doesn't work, then stop trying. Finding someone or something else to take the place of what you wanted in the first place might make you decide that it wasn't so important after all.

BEING GOOD WON'T WORK MAGIC

But some kids are not willing to give up what they want. They want to be in control, like a magician.

They think, "Mom and Dad got divorced because I was bad. So it makes sense that if I'm good they will get back together again." If you have thoughts like these, you need to know some important facts.

Being good won't work magic. It won't bring your parents together again. Your parents didn't get divorced because you were bad. All kids do bad things sometimes, like making a mess, or hitting their brothers or sisters. These things don't make parents get divorced. Divorce is a grownup problem. It's not your fault!

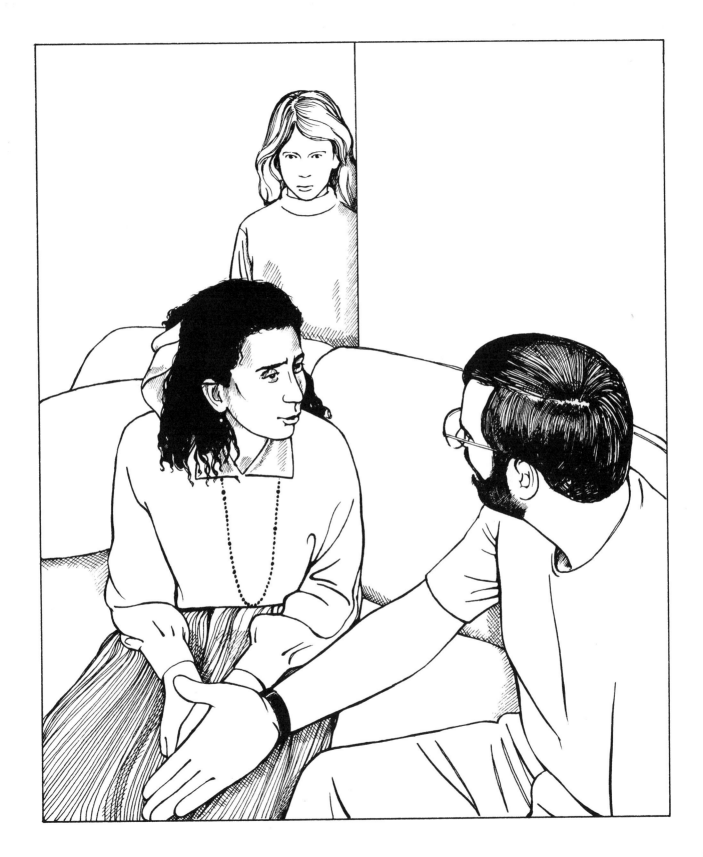

Sometimes kids think divorce is their fault because they don't want to believe that it's their parents' fault. Kids count on their parents to take care of them, so they're scared to think their parents might make mistakes. But guess what? Everybody makes mistakes sometimes—even parents.

Your parents may think that it was a mistake for them to marry each other. But just because they think their marriage was a mistake doesn't mean that you can't have a happy marriage of your own someday.

DON'T PLAY THE BLAMING GAME

You should also remember that it's a waste of time thinking about who's to blame for the divorce. Maybe that's just what your mom and dad are doing—playing the blaming game. Your mom says it's your dad's fault. Your dad says it's your mom's fault.

And you're right in the middle, feeling like you have to choose. But you don't have to play this game, and you shouldn't, because you can't win it—no one can.

If your mom or dad says mean stuff about the other, tell them to stop, that you don't want to hear that stuff. Remember that you can still love both your parents, and there's no reason why their divorce has to change your feelings about either one of them.

If one parent tries to make you think that you have to like the other parent, then you'll need to tell them that they are not allowed to make you take sides.

Let them know that they are not allowed to use you as a messenger. After all, they are grownups, and grownups should know how to talk with each other. They are not allowed to use you as a tattle-tale or spy. No one likes tattle-tales, and being a spy may be neat on TV, but it's not in this case!

SOME DIVORCE "DOS AND DON'TS"

Here are some more hints on how to make things feel more normal again.

Act your real age. Now that your mom is alone, you may have to help with some grownup jobs around the house, like babysitting and cleaning, and that's just fine. You can feel proud of yourself for being grownup enough to help out.

If you're a boy, don't try to take your dad's place around your mom. If you're a girl, don't try to take your mom's place around your dad.

And don't act like a baby either! Some kids try to get extra attention after a divorce by acting like they're helpless. Some moms and dads go along with this and treat their kids like they're much younger than they really are. But the best thing parents can do for their children is to help them grow and mature naturally.

Don't think of your mom as "Mean Old Mom" and your dad as "Mr. Nice Guy." If you live with your mom, during the week she is the one who will help you with the boring stuff, like doing homework and getting ready for school. Because your dad probably only sees you on weekends, he may do fun stuff with you like going to the movies or out for pizza.

Rather than blame your mom for making you do the boring stuff, ask her to set aside some special time for just the two of you. You don't have to do anything exciting—the two of you can just spend five minutes alone together, talking about what you both did during the day and the feelings you both had.

It's important for you and your dad to have time like this too. Like most fathers, your dad may feel bad about his divorce, and very sorry that he is not living with you.

Because of these feelings, he may try to spoil you. He may want to do lots of fancy things with you. Let him know that regular activities are okay with you too. Let him know that it's fine with you to play in his yard, watch TV, and just plain be with him.

Going back and forth between your mom's and dad's homes can be pretty confusing. To make sure that both homes feel like home to you, here are a couple of ideas.

Keep your own calendar, and ask one of your parents to help you mark the days you'll be with your mom and the days you'll be with your dad.

Keep a few of your favorite toys at each parent's home. That way, no matter which roof you're under, the last thing you'll see before you close your eyes at night will be something that's special to you.

APRIL

Sun	Mon	Tue	Wed	Thur	Fri	Sat
			1	2	3	4 See dad
5 See dad	6	7	8 dentist	9	10	11
12	13	14	15	16 big game today	17	18 See dad
19 dad	20	21	22	23	24 visit grandma	25
26	27	28	29	30		

Your family is going through a lot of changes because of your parents' divorce. Remember that it's important to keep talking about how you feel about these changes with your mom, your dad and with any other grownups you love and trust. Expressing your feelings will help you help yourself, and pretty soon your "new life" won't feel new or different at all.

TWENTY VERY IMPORTANT THINGS TO REMEMBER

1. Divorce is never, ever the child's fault. Divorce is hardly ever one parent's fault.

2. Your mom will always be your mom, and your dad will always be your dad, no matter where they live, whether they live with you or not.

3. Nothing is wrong with you just because your mom and dad are divorced.

4. A child can almost always live with one parent or another. If he can't, there will always be someone to care for him.

5. Even if a parent doesn't live with you anymore, he or she can still love you.

6. Never think that your parents will get back together if you are on your best behavior. One thing has nothing to do with the other.

7. It's OK to cry! And you'll feel better if you do.

8. It's OK to get angry! Anger can be expressed in a positive way.

9. If you feel angry or sad, tell someone! You'll feel better, and that person will too, because you have trusted him.

10. Your feelings of anger and sadness will bother you less and less. It just takes time.

11. Never be afraid to ask questions about divorce if something is puzzling you. There are many good listeners who care about you and will want to help you.

12. Just because your parents think that it was a mistake for them to marry each other doesn't mean that you can't have a happy marriage of your own someday.

13. Never let your parents put you in the middle of their problems, and never let them use you as a messenger.

14. Never be afraid or embarrassed to tell your friends that your parents aren't living together anymore.

15. Don't feel guilty if you are having a good time with your friends while your mom or dad is feeling bad. It's OK to feel good when others aren't.

16. If you have a lawyer, he or she is on your side, like a friend would be.

17. If you have a therapist or social worker, you need to tell her what you are feeling so that she can help you feel better.

18. Thinking up ways to get your parent back together won't make them do it.

19. Don't be like the dog who barked up the wrong tree—it's a waste of time to wish you had your "old" life back.

20. Before you know it, your "new" life will be as familiar to you as your "old" life was.

DIVORCE WORDS AND WHAT THEY MEAN

alimony
The money that one parent—usually the dad—pays the other parent after a divorce.

alternating custody
When a child lives with one parent for a period of time and the other parent for another period of time.

broken home
An old-fashioned term for families wherein the parents have divorced or separated. Few people use this expression anymore because divorce means "change" - nothing really "breaks."

child support
The money that one parent—usually the dad—pays the other parent to help take care of their children.

custody arrangements
Rules about which parent is responsible for taking care of you. Usually both parents help make important decisions like where you'll live and go to school. But the parent with custody has the final say.

divorce

A process that married people go through to legally end a marriage.

divorce decree

The document that says two people are no longer married.

family therapist/psychiatrist/psychologist/social worker

A person who is trained to help people sort things out when they're having problems.

grounds for divorce

The legal reason people get divorced.

guardian

A relative, close friend or adult other than the parent who has custody of a child.

joint custody

When a mom and dad share equally in the responsibility of taking care of you even though they are divorced.

judge

A person who helps make fair decisions about your parents' divorce. In court, the judge wears a long black robe that may look scary. But this robe is just a uniform. The judge is there to help.

lawyer

A man or woman who helps your mom and dad understand the laws or rules about divorce. The lawyer can also take your side and represent you, your mom or your dad in court.

mediation

When parents try to agree on things about their divorce. When they do this, they get another grownup called a mediator to help them. They still need to get a judge to write it all down. Many parents are happiest when they can work out their divorce in a friendly way.

reconciliation

When parents who are separated decide to live together again.

sole custody

When one parent cares for a child almost all of the time.

visitation arrangements

Rules about when you'll stay with each of your parents. There are many different kinds of arrangements that work for different families.

WHAT WOULD <u>YOU</u> SAY?

Ten scenes in which children can write the words and feelings of the characters.

TELL-A-STORY PAGES

Six "story starters" for children to finish with their own endings.

Tim woke up one sunny morning...

_____

_____

_____

_____

_____

_____

_____

_____

_____

_____

_____

_____

_____

_____

_____

_____

Ellen's father had planned a special day...

_____

_____

_____

_____

_____

_____

_____

_____

_____

_____

_____

_____

_____

_____

_____

_____

_____

Maurice knew that things would go his way today...

_____

_____

_____

_____

_____

_____

_____

_____

_____

_____

_____

_____

_____

_____

_____

Sylvie's smile brightened up the classroom...

_____

_____

_____

_____

_____

_____

_____

_____

_____

_____

_____

_____

_____

_____

_____

_____

_____

Robert's mom said, "I'm so proud of you…"

_____

_____

_____

_____

_____

_____

_____

_____

_____

_____

_____

_____

_____

_____

_____

Linda came home with her best report card ever and everyone...

_____

_____

_____

_____

_____

_____

_____

_____

_____

_____

_____

_____

_____

_____

_____

_____

_____

_____

ABOUT THE AUTHOR

Mary Blitzer Field holds an MA in English Literature from Columbia University and teaches writing and literature at Villanova University. Currently residing near Philadelphia, she writes for a variety of medical and psychological publications. The daughter of a psychoanalyst, the wife of a psychologist and the mother of two school-aged children, she brings a special perspective to bear on topics relating to child psychology.

ABOUT THE CONCEPT

The Play-and-Read Series was developed by child psychologist Lawrence E. Shapiro, Ph.D. Dr. Shapiro is the author of over a dozen books and therapeutic games. He is the founder and president of The Center for Applied Psychology, Inc. and Childswork/Childsplay, the nation's largest distributor of psychologically-oriented toys, games, and books, based in King of Prussia, Pennsylvania. The Play-and-Read Series was developed by Dr. Shapiro to help children express themselves through their most natural language–imaginative play.